LAWMEN OF
THE OLD WEST

JAMES L. COLLINS

LAWMEN

OF THE OLD WEST

Franklin Watts
New York/London/Toronto/Sydney
A First Book/1990

Cover photo courtesy of Thomas Gilcrease Institute, Tulsa, Oklahoma.
Map by Joe Le Monnier
Photographs courtesy of:
Amon Carter Museum, Fort Worth: p. 10; The Bancroft
Library, University of California, Berkeley: p. 13;
Kansas State Historical Society, Topeka: pp. 20, 24 (both);
Thomas Gilcrease Institute, Tulsa, Oklahoma: pp. 23, 55;
Western History Collections, University of Oklahoma Library:
pp. 29, 31, 34, 40, 42, 51; New York Public Library
Picture Collection: pp. 33, 37 (both), 44, 47, 52, 57;
Historical Pictures Service: p. 49.

Library of Congress Cataloging-in-Publication Data

Collins, James L., 1945–
Lawmen of the Old West / by James L. Collins.
p.   cm. — (A First book)
Summary: An examination of the roles of law enforcement agents
in frontier towns of the old West.
ISBN 0-531-10893-7
1. Peace officers—West (U.S.)—History—19th century—Juvenile
literature. 2. West (U.S.)—History—1848–1950—Juvenile literature.
3. Frontier and pioneer life—West (U.S.)—Juvenile literature. [1.
Peace officers—West (U.S.) 2. West (U.S.)—History—1848–1950.
3. Frontier and pioneer life—West (U.S.)] I. Title. II. Series.
F596.C73   1990
978'.02—dc20   89-22555   CIP   AC

This book is dedicated first to
my mother, who very much deserves it
just for being my mother, second to
my Uncle Frank, who, when I was ten,
gave me my first book to read and
still remains in my memory, and last
but not least, to the rest of those
Malde girls, who certainly deserve
mention in a frontier book like this.

CONTENTS

LAWMEN OF
THE OLD WEST

The Old West was a place where guns reigned.

PREFACE

Lawmen of the West! Just hearing these words brings about a certain feeling of adventure. A vision of tall, lean men who were fast with a gun and could fight the very devil himself if called on to do so. Marshals, sheriffs, and rangers. All these men worked hard to keep the settlers of the West safe from rustlers and horse thieves, bank and stage-coach robbers, and a host of others. They were men who were looked up to with admiration and respect.

Well, most of them were. The truth of the matter is that as much as these men were heroes in their own right, they were also as tough as the men they put in jail. Sometimes they were tougher. Sometimes they were not honest either. It is sad to say that some of these people were downright crooked. A number of them, like "Wild Bill" Hickok and Wyatt Earp, both Kansas lawmen, made more money at the card table gambling than they did from their monthly salaries as town marshals. They were professional gamblers as much as they were professional lawmen.

It is easy to see why there is so much controversy about many of the lawmen of the West. "Wild Bill" Hickok, in particular, is viewed as a "mankiller" by many of his biographers. This is true, for he did indeed kill a number of men. What is so often overlooked about men such as Hickok is that, as deadly as he was, he did not go looking for trouble. As a lawman, he only responded to the call of duty, protecting himself and the town citizens. "Wild Bill" Hickok was not a "bad man," but rather a "bad man to tangle with." There is a difference. A "bad man" was a thief or a robber, or just a plain bully. But a "bad man to tangle with" was a man who was as deadly as a coiled rattlesnake! Hickok, "Bat" Masterson, and "Texas John" Slaughter were just a few of the men who had reputations for being "bad men to tangle with," and each man deserved that reputation.

Still, they were a breed of men who were necessary to make life on the frontier safe. When they met you on the street, they would look you over and

*Despite the presence of lawmen on the
frontier, some people took justice into
their own hands. With the white-haired man
on the left in charge, these settlers try
an accused horse thief (standing, center).*

[13]

ask what your business was in town. If they liked you and didn't figure you for trouble, why, they might even remember you!

Here's hoping the stories in this book will be just as entertaining to you now as meeting these lawmen of the West in person would have been over a century ago.

THE TOWN MARSHAL

If ever there was a man who had a responsible position, it was the town marshal on the frontier we call the Old West. His position has been glorified in thousands of motion pictures and Western novels. As the man behind the badge, he was charged with keeping the peace in a rough-and-tumble cowtown. Well, that is true as far as it goes.

It is true that the marshals who wore their badges in the cowtowns of Ellsworth, Abilene, Wichita, and Dodge City, to name but a few, had their work cut out for them and earned every bit of their pay. But these lawmen didn't exist in just the cowtowns of Kansas or the mining towns of Colorado or Nevada. Every town that sprouted up west of the Missouri after the end of the Civil War (1865) sooner or later

C

Seattle

WASHINGTON
(1889)

Ft. Benten

Portland

Helena

MONTANA

OREGON

IDAHO
(1890)

WYOMING
(1890)

Ft. Fetterman

Ft. Lara

Ogden

Cheyenn

Sacramento

Virginia City

NEVADA

Salt
Lake City

San Fransisco

COLORADO
(1876)

UTAH
TERRITORY

Leadville

Denve

Colora
Sprinc

Ouray

Silverton

Pueb

Telluride

CALIFORNIA

ARIZONA
TERRITORY

Santa Fe

Los Angeles

Thomas Rynning

Albuquerque

"Cap" Mossman

San Diego

Ft. Yuma

"Texas John" Slaughter

NEW MEXICO
TERRITORY

Pat (

Tucson

Lincoln County

Tombstone

El Paso

MEXICO

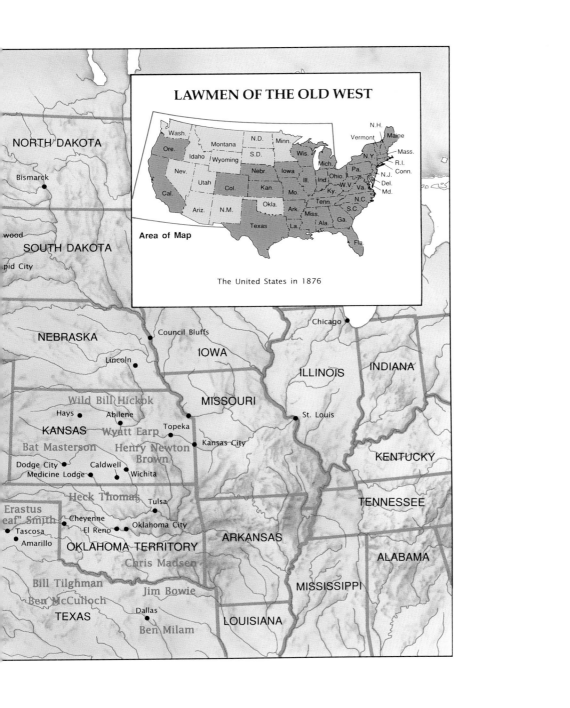

NORTH DAKOTA

Bismarck

wood

SOUTH DAKOTA

pid City

LAWMEN OF THE OLD WEST

Wash.
Ore.
Idaho
Nev.
Cal.
Utah
Ariz.
N.M.
Montana
Wyoming
S.D.
Nebr.
Col.
Kan.
Okla.
Texas
N.D.
Minn.
Wis.
Iowa
Ill.
Mo.
Ark.
Miss.
La.
Mich.
Ohio.
Ind.
Ky.
Tenn.
Ala.
Ga.
Fla.
N.H.
Vermont
Maine
Mass.
N.Y.
Pa.
R.I.
Conn.
N.J.
Del.
Md.
W.V.
Va.
N.C.
S.C.

Area of Map

The United States in 1876

Chicago

NEBRASKA

Council Bluffs

IOWA

Lincoln

Wild Bill Hickok

Hays   Abilene

Topeka

KANSAS   Wyatt Earp

Kansas City

Bat Masterson   Henry Newton Brown

Dodge City   Caldwell

Medicine Lodge   Wichita

MISSOURI

St. Louis

ILLINOIS

INDIANA

KENTUCKY

Heck Thomas   Tulsa

Erastus
eaf" Smith   Cheyenne

Tascosa   El Reno   Oklahoma City

Amarillo

OKLAHOMA TERRITORY

ARKANSAS

TENNESSEE

Chris Madsen

ALABAMA

Bill Tilghman   Jim Bowie

MISSISSIPPI

Ben McCulloch

Dallas

TEXAS   LOUISIANA

Ben Milam

had a lawman to keep the peace, and he was usually a town marshal.

Bravery and courage have always been requirements for becoming a lawman, whether a full-time marshal or a part-time deputy. Being good with a six-gun and a rifle was handy too. But perhaps the most important quality a lawman could have was good old horse sense. Remember that the lawman of the Old West often had to be self-reliant in administering their duties. Not all of them knew the laws of the county or territory in which they lived, but most could remember the difference between right and wrong their parents had taught them. Remember too that the lawmen of the Old West lived in a time when a six-gun and rifle were available to nearly everyone. Although carrying a six-gun was normal in this unsettled land, it could also be dangerous if tempers flared and someone decided to settle an argument with a gun. It was up to the lawman and his deputies to see that such things did not happen.

Normally, the town marshal served as the chief-of-police and was appointed by the community mayor and his town council—who could fire him whenever they were dissatisfied with his performance, or lack of it. The marshal would usually appoint an assistant marshal, or deputy, and a handful of policemen to assist him. He also had the authority to call upon the local citizens for assistance in case of an emergency. Such an emergency might be a bank robbery by half a dozen men. Although the town marshal's jurisdiction ended at the city limits, an imaginary boundary never kept a dozen angry town citizens from hunting down the bank robbers and hanging them from the nearest tree without the presence of judge or jury. The pay for this job typically started at $50 a month and went up to about $250, depending on the marshal's reputation.

Often it would take a very tough man to take the job of town marshal. This is where men like James Butler "Wild Bill" Hickok (May 27, 1837–August 2,1876) and Wyatt Earp (March 19, 1848–January 13, 1929) came into play. Two of the more famous frontier marshals, both men had reputations as "gunmen" who were good with a six-gun and brave and fearless to a fault. It is this kind of man who has so often been portrayed as the hard, tough but fair lawman in Western novels, movies, and television.

Hickok and Earp had similar lives and careers before becoming Kansas lawmen. Although eleven years separated the two in age, both were born in Illinois and raised on farms. Both had held jobs with the stage lines and worked as scouts in one capacity or another, finally serving as town marshals in the years from 1869 to 1879.

"Bear River" Tom Smith, the marshal of Abilene, Kansas, where the great Texas cattle trade was centered. He was killed in a cave while trying to arrest some outlaws.

While Hickok was appointed marshal of Hays, Kansas, in 1869, it was his short but effective tour as town marshal of Abilene, Kansas, in 1871, that added to his reputation as "prince of the pistoleers." In 1870, Abilene was in its heyday as a cowtown. The town had been kept safe that summer during the arrival of the Texas trail drives by "Bear River" Tom Smith, a big man who served as marshal and proved that he was faster with his fists than his guns. But Marshal Smith never saw the end of the year, for he was killed on November 2, 1870, while serving a warrant on a man outside Abilene who had been charged with a killing.

Word got back to Texas that spring that the Texans would be dealing with "Wild Bill" Hickok rather than "Bear River" Tom Smith at trail's end during the summer of 1871. Hickok was totally different from Smith in that he used his guns to win a fight and hadn't lost a fight yet. Although the Texans disliked Hickok—he was a Yankee to begin with—they had great respect for his reputation as a bad man to tangle with, and their stay in Abilene was peaceful for the most part. Only one incident took place that fall, and it devastated Hickok.

On October 5, 1871, some rowdy Texans who had stayed in town after the cattle drive began to cause a commotion in front of the Alamo Saloon. Hickok got wind of the trouble and was there immediately. On his way over he heard a shot. He picked out a Texas gambler by the name of Phil Coe as the leader of the mob. When Hickok asked about the fired shot, Coe said he had shot a dog, but no dog was in sight.

Surrounded by more than three dozen Texans, Hickok was a cautious man, his gun now drawn. He suddenly heard a man to his rear shouting his name and, thinking it to be another Texan, turned and shot

[21]

him dead. The man was his good friend Mike Williams, who had been coming to Hickok's aid. At the same time, Phil Coe thought he had a chance to kill Hickok and began firing at the marshal. His shots only tore up Hickok's coat, while Hickok planted two shots in Coe's stomach, mortally wounding him. (Coe died three days later.) Hickok was so furious at having mistakenly killed his friend that it took him only one hour to go through every saloon in town and drive out, single-handedly, all the Texans.

"Wild Bill" Hickok was so devastated by the death of his friend that he never again held the position of lawman. However, his reputation as a gunman continued to spread until his death in Deadwood, the Dakota Territory, on August 2, 1876, when he was shot in the back by "Broken Nose" Jack McCall.

In the same year that Hickok died, Wyatt Earp's career as a Kansas lawman started. Earp was far different from Hickok. Where Hickok's reputation was built on deeds that were witnessed, Earp became a legend in his own time largely due to his own imagination. Earp claimed to be the one who bravely stepped forward and arrested gunman Ben Thompson in Ellsworth after Thompson's brother, Billy, shot and killed Sheriff Chauncy B. Whitney. No record exists to prove this claim true.

One of the best-known of the western lawmen, "Wild Bill" Hickok came to symbolize the lawman as hero. He was born in Illinois and went to Kansas as a young man. As well as being a marshal, Hickok was a professional gambler.

Wyatt Earp (right) was an admired and respected peace officer. Below: sometimes lawmen themselves got into trouble. Town marshal Henry Brown (center), the assistant marshal Ben Wheeler (right), and two others robbed a bank in Kansas.

According to the newspapers of the day, Earp did an effective job of serving as a policeman in Wichita (1874–1875) and occasional deputy city marshal of Dodge City from 1876 to 1879. But the only real fame he can lay claim to was his participation in the well-known gunfight at OK Corral, where he took part in the killing of Tom and Frank McLaury and Billy Clanton. Although it is quite likely that Wyatt Earp killed Frank Stilwell and Florentino Cruz in the following year for the murder of his brother, Morgan Earp, it is highly unlikely that he killed ''Curly Bill'' Brocious, as he claimed.

Sometimes the town fathers didn't care if a man had run afoul of the law in some other territory, just so long as he could do his job in their town. Thus was the case in Caldwell, Kansas, in 1882, when Henry Newton Brown (1857–1884) joined the police force as an assistant marshal and, within a year's time, was made the marshal. Brown had ridden with Billy the Kid during the Lincoln County War of 1878 and had served as constable of Tascosa, one of the toughest Southwestern towns, before drifting up to Caldwell. But he gained the respect of the community in Caldwell by killing two men in the line of duty over a two-year period. It was when Brown and two friends held up the bank of Medicine Lodge, Kansas, not far from Caldwell, that everyone was surprised. Brown and his friends killed two men during the holdup, but they were caught, jailed, and hanged by a lynch mob when they tried to escape.

Perhaps the best that can be said of these men came from one of their own, who said that "these men served society fearlessly and with inadequate reward, and resorted to guns only in reluctant self-defense."

THE SHERIFF

The next step up in the hierarchy of the lawmen of the West is the county sheriff, who was responsible for law and order in the county. His jurisdiction started at the city limits of the town, where the town marshal's authority ended. Like the town marshal's position, the sheriff's position was modeled on the law officials of England. The sheriff was normally elected to office every two years. Yet he rarely had much to do with criminals at large and left a good deal of this work to his under sheriff and deputies.

Depending on the size of the county, the sheriff could also be charged with collecting county taxes, often taking a percentage of what he collected as a fee. All sheriffs were charged with maintaining the county jail, serving court orders, and selling the property of people who didn't pay their taxes. They might also have some rather odd duties to perform. For instance, in Wyoming, sheriffs inspected the owners' brands on all horses that were to be driven out of the state, to guard against theft. Utah's sheriffs maintained not only the county jails but also the county dog pounds. In Colorado, sheriffs helped fight forest fires; in Texas, they helped to get rid of prairie dogs; and in New Mexico, they searched for straying livestock.

These old-time sheriffs were usually paid between $200 and $500 per month, depending on how rich the county was and how much the county commissioner was prepared to pay. This seems like a lot of money to pay a man who was largely a figurehead and administrator, but then a county was much larger than a town and had a bigger territory to cover. The under sheriff got approximately half the sheriff's salary, and the deputies received about two-thirds the under sheriff's salary. Except for the top job, law enforcement was rarely well paid in those days.

There were a number of famous men who held the office of sheriff during this time. In the same years that Wyatt Earp spent his summers as marshal of Dodge City (1877–1879), his good friend, William B. ("Bat") Masterson (November 26, 1853–October

Bat Masterson, sheriff of Ford County, Kansas, became a sportswriter for a New York newspaper.

25, 1921), served as sheriff of the surrounding Ford County. The two of them managed to keep the peace in Dodge City and Ford County while they were in office.

Bat Masterson first came to prominence when, on July 27, 1874, he was included as one of the twenty-eight buffalo hunters who made a stand at the Second Battle of Adobe Walls on the Canadian River in the Northern Texas Panhandle. The buffalo hunters suddenly found themselves all but over-whelmed by nearly one thousand Comanche, Southern Apache, Kiowa, and Cheyenne Indians. But they stood their ground for the better part of a week and lost only one man in the battle.

Masterson turned out to be one of the more active sheriffs to take office. As sheriff of Ford County, he gained fame by leading posses after, and catching, a variety of killers, thieves, and ruffians.

Bat Masterson was known as a bad man to tangle with and went on to become a sports writer for a New York newspaper later in his life. But his exploits as sheriff of Ford County on the frontier of Kansas are certainly his most memorable experiences.

One of the most famous sheriffs of the Southwest was Patrick Floyd Garrett (June 5, 1850–February 29, 1908). Like many of the men of his day, Pat Garrett was a tall, striking individual who had a look of authority about him. The event in his life for which he is best known involved perhaps the hardest decision he ever had to make.

Garrett's story goes hand in hand with the most famous gunman and outlaw of the Southwest, Billy the Kid. The two met after Garrett moved to Lincoln, New Mexico, in 1879. Lincoln County had just gone through a range war, in which Billy the Kid took part. The Kid had gained a reputation as a tough young man of nineteen, who had killed a handful of men during that armed conflict. But after the Lincoln County War was over, Billy the Kid turned to a life of crime and was accused of stealing cattle, among other things. How much truth there is to this has

Of the three noted sheriffs of Lincoln County, New Mexico, Pat Garrett (left) was the most famous.

always been debated. A warrant was sworn out for the arrest of Billy the Kid, but the Kid managed to evade every lawman who came after him. That is, until Pat Garrett was elected sheriff of Lincoln County in 1880 and was put in charge of bringing in Billy the Kid.

Pat Garrett and Billy the Kid had become friends as soon as they had met. Because of their size, Garrett being tall and lanky and the Kid being a bit on the short side, they became known as "Big Casino" and "Little Casino." But Garrett knew he represented the law in Lincoln County and, after a long manhunt, he captured Billy the Kid. Jailed in Lincoln to await trial, Billy successfully broke out of jail, killing two guards.

Another man might have had second thoughts about going after a gunman as dangerous as Billy the Kid, but not Pat Garrett. He knew the importance of his job and set out to hunt down the man who was once his friend. On the night of July 14, 1881, Sheriff Pat Garrett caught up with Billy the Kid at Pete Maxwell's ranch and shot him dead. Few people have ever had to track down and kill a friend, so one can only imagine how difficult it must have been to choose between carrying out the letter of the law and sparing a friend.

While the New Mexico Territory had Pat Garrett

*Garrett's most noteworthy experience involved
his relationship with and capture of the notorious
outlaw, Billy the Kid. This drawing from Garrett's
biography depicts the death of Billy.*

Former sheriff John Slaughter at his San Bernardino ranch in Arizona in 1915 with some of his cattle.

as a famous sheriff, the Arizona Territory had John Horton ("Texas John") Slaughter (October 2, 1841–February 15, 1922). Although he had severe asthma and stood only 5′6″ tall, John Slaughter was an excellent example of a man who firmly believed that the courage within a man should be his driving force.

In 1886, at the age of forty-five, John Slaughter was elected sheriff of Colchise County. The county was fast becoming a haven for rustlers and stagecoach robbers. Slaughter, who had once been a Texas Ranger, loaded his ten-gauge shotgun with buckshot and issued an ultimatum to the outlaws of the territory: "Get out or get shot." During his two terms as sheriff, he is said to have killed some twelve men, who found out the hard way that "Texas John" Slaughter was a bad man to tangle with.

After cleaning up the territory, Slaughter retired to his ranch in 1890. But in 1895 the former sheriff received a deputy's commission, which he held until his death in 1922.

It was almost impossible for one man to clean up the territory entirely. So it is best to say that these men made it safer for people to live in the counties they served. These sheriffs also laid a strong foundation for the qualities this type of lawman should have—they were strong, silent, capable, and, when the time called for it, quite deadly.

THE UNITED STATES MARSHAL

Of all the lawmen of the Old West, the most respected was the United States marshal. The position
of marshal was officially created in 1789, and the
country once again looked to England for an example
of a lawman who would represent the United States
government.

The higher up you got in the hierarchy of the
lawman, the more political the system became. In
other words, courage and honesty weren't as necessary for an appointment to a federal position as
was one's political viewpoint. Since a United States
marshal was appointed by the president of the
United States and confirmed by the Congress, the
appointed marshals might change as often as the
administration changed. Perhaps this is why such

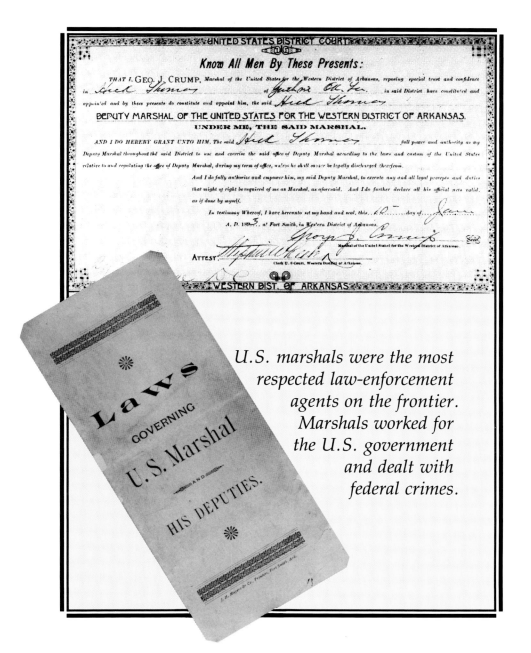

UNITED STATES DISTRICT COURT

Know All Men By These Presents:

THAT I, GEO. J. CRUMP, Marshal of the United States for the Western District of Arkansas, reposing special trust and confidence in _____ of _____ in said District have constituted and appointed and by these presents do constitute and appoint him, the said _____

DEPUTY MARSHAL OF THE UNITED STATES FOR THE WESTERN DISTRICT OF ARKANSAS.

UNDER ME, THE SAID MARSHAL.

AND I DO HEREBY GRANT UNTO HIM, The said _____ full power and authority as my Deputy Marshal throughout the said District to use and exercise the said office of Deputy Marshal according to the laws and custom of the United States relative to and regulating the office of Deputy Marshal, during my term of office, unless he shall sooner be legally discharged therefrom.

And I do fully authorize and empower him, my said Deputy Marshal, to execute any and all legal precepts and duties that might of right be required of me as Marshal, as aforesaid. And I do further declare all his official acts valid, as if done by myself.

In testimony Whereof, I have hereunto set my hand and seal, this 10___ day of _____ A. D. 189_, at Fort Smith, in Western District of Arkansas.

_____ [Seal]

Marshal of the United States for the Western District of Arkansas.

ATTEST: _____

Clerk U. S. Court, Western District of Arkansas.

WESTERN DIST. OF ARKANSAS

Laws
GOVERNING
U.S. Marshal
AND
HIS DEPUTIES.

U.S. marshals were the most respected law-enforcement agents on the frontier. Marshals worked for the U.S. government and dealt with federal crimes.

men were sometimes involved in fraud and embezzlement schemes.

Much of the land west of the Missouri River after the Civil War was divided into large territories. It wasn't impossible for a United States marshal to be put in charge of tens of thousands of square miles. This was a huge responsibility that usually required a large number of deputy United States marshals for the actual performance of duties.

Many of the deputy U.S. marshals were also local lawmen. For example, "Wild Bill" Hickok and Wyatt Earp were both town marshals, and at one time or another during their careers they were also appointed deputy U.S. marshals. Sheriffs could also be appointed deputy U.S. marshals.

Until 1896, when the law was changed, the U.S. marshal and his deputies were paid a onetime fee rather than a continuing salary. The idea behind this was that the fee could be large or small, depending on how active the marshal and his deputies were in bringing in those who broke the law. For those local lawmen who also served as federal lawmen, such a fee served to supplement the usually meager salary they drew.

The duties of the U.S. marshal were mainly concerned with federal crimes, desertion from the Army, and crimes committed on Indian reservations. But federal marshals didn't have to wait for a crime to take place. These men could also be summoned to duty if there was a threat of a federal law being broken. Thus, they could often act as guards for the mails and railroad property. Nor did such men have a boundary, like the town marshal or county sheriff. In more than one case, deputy U.S. marshals were known to have chased train robbers over several territories before catching them.

Among the more famous deputy U.S. marshals were a trio of men known in Oklahoma as "The Three Guardsmen." Although they seldom rode together, these three men did more than their share to bring law and order to the Oklahoma Territory.

Christian ("Chris") Madsen (February 25, 1851–January 9, 1944) was born in Denmark and didn't come to the United States until 1876. He immediately joined the U.S. Cavalry and spent fifteen years soldiering in the West. In 1891 he resigned from the service as a sergeant and recipient of a Silver Star, and accepted an appointment as deputy U.S. marshal, operating out of El Reno, Oklahoma.

One of Madsen's more famous arrest attempts was on March 5, 1896, near Cheyenne, Oklahoma. Madsen was after "Red Buck" George Weightman, who had been a vicious member of both the Dalton and Doolin gangs. When Madsen caught up with

Chris Madsen had been one of Custer's scouts and had been left for dead on the battlefield at Wounded Knee. He later became a deputy United States marshal.

Weightman, the outlaw tried to shoot his way out of a dugout he was hidden in, but Madsen killed him with a rifle shot.

Madsen joined Teddy Roosevelt's Rough Riders when the Spanish-American War began in 1898, and he returned to law enforcement after the war. He was appointed United States marshal for Oklahoma in 1911.

William Matthew ("Billy") Tilghman, Jr. (July 4, 1854–November 1, 1924) had been a deputy sheriff and city marshal before being appointed a deputy U.S. marshal in 1892. Tilghman spent two decades curbing outlaws in the Oklahoma Territory before being elected to the state senate.

Billy Tilghman proved himself to be a man of iron nerve, but one who also had a sense of humor in a job normally quite serious. In 1894, Tilghman was with another lawman in search of two teen age girls in the Doolin gang, Jennie ("Little Britches") Stevens and "Cattle Annie" McDougal. When they found the pair, Tilghman's partner captured Cattle Annie, while he went after Little Britches. Tilghman had no desire to kill the fleeing girl, so he shot her horse out from under her and promptly treated her like his own daughter. He spanked her.

The next year, 1895, Tilghman tracked down Bill Doolin of the deadly Dalton gang, near Eureka Springs, Arkansas. Wearing a long black coat and looking like a minister, Tilghman confronted the unsuspecting Doolin and convinced him that surrendering was better than dying.

The third of "The Three Guardsmen" was Henry Andrew ("Heck") Thomas (January 6, 1850–August 11, 1912), who was born and raised in Georgia. Like Madsen and Tilghman, Thomas had a tough reputation before he was asked to accept an appointment as a deputy U.S. marshal in the Oklahoma Territory

in 1893. In fact, it was in 1893 that Madsen, Tilghman, and Thomas formed their trio. They would spend the better part of three years hunting down the famous Dalton gang. It was during this three-year period (1893–1896) that Heck Thomas arrested more than three hundred wanted men.

The same Bill Doolin whom Billy Tilghman had arrested and taken into custody met a less compassionate man in Heck Thomas. Within a month after his capture, Doolin escaped from jail. But Thomas got a tip on where Doolin was headed and surprised him at his father-in-law's ranch. When Thomas told Doolin to surrender, the outlaw began shooting at the lawman. By the time a rifle and pistol were shot from his hands, Doolin had been filled with twenty-one bullet holes and was dead.

"Cattle Annie" and "Little Britches," members of Oklahoma outlaw gangs, were captured by U.S. Marshal Bill Tilghman. They were both sent to reform school.

Lawmen such as the United States marshal and his deputies had to be very aware of their limitations. Since they officially belonged to no state, they couldn't be tried for any murders they committed. It was all too easy for a man to let the position and power go to his head. But, although it was tempting, a federal lawman just couldn't behave in such a way. As romanticized as the job has become in Western novels and films, the man who wore that famed star had to be cool and level-headed.

Deputy U.S. Marshal Heck Thomas (left), shown here with a fellow lawman, two Indian scouts, and two court officers, was a fearless lawman who was shot and wounded several times in gun battles.

THE RANGERS

The story goes that a tall, lanky young man rode into a south Texas town and reported to the mayor. The town, it seems, was having troubles that were about to bring it to the brink of a riot. The town council and mayor had decided to call in the Texas Rangers to stop the riot before it got started. But the mayor was puzzled when he found out the young man was a Texas Ranger.

"They only sent *one* ranger to take care of the riot?" he asked in disbelief.

The young ranger shrugged. "You've only got one riot, don't you?"

This is one of the numerous stories that make it sound as though the Texas Rangers could do just about anything to keep the peace in Texas, no matter

The Texas Rangers helped keep law and order in the Texas Territory when local officials needed assistance. They could travel anywhere in the state.

what the odds. In many cases, this was closer to truth than fiction.

It isn't certain just when the Texas Rangers came into being. Stephen Austin, who colonized Texas in 1823, was known to have issued an order to have a group of "rangers" on hand to deal with unfriendly Mexicans and the Comanche Indians. By 1835, when Texas had decided to fight for its independence, the Texas Rangers became a legal force. Such well-known Texans as Jim Bowie, Erastus "Deaf" Smith, and Ben Milam were rangers during the Texas war of independence.

The Texas Ranger was never subject to military regulation. Nor was he subject to local law, because he could go from one end of the state of Texas to the other in order to carry out his duties. He wore no uniform. His purpose was to maintain or restore order in situations that got beyond the control of local officers but were not serious enough to justify military force. In the early years, before the Civil War, Texas Rangers operated against Indian and Mexican raiders. Later they operated against outlaw bands, feudists, livestock thieves, and local rioters.

The Texas Ranger was paid $25 per month. He provided his own horse, saddle, pistol, and knife—the state provided a rifle. For the sum of $25 a month, the Texas Ranger was expected to be able to "ride like

James Bowie was one of the better-known Texas Rangers. Rangers helped restore order in many situations, such as during a railroad strike.

a Mexican, trail like an Indian, shoot like a Tennessean, and fight like the very devil," according to John S. "Rip" Ford, one of the best-known Texas Rangers.

The Texas Rangers fought bravely in the Mexican War (1846–1848). Ben McCulloch, one of the best-known rangers of that period, volunteered his ranger force for service with the Confederacy when the Civil War began. As a brigadier general, he was killed in the Battle of Elk Horn on March 7, 1862.

The Texas Rangers were temporarily disbanded during the Civil War. They were called back to service in 1874, after the Reconstruction period had brought about much feuding and thievery in Texas. For sixteen years, the rangers fought organized gangs of rustlers and horse thieves, as well as bank and stagecoach robbers. By 1890 the Texas frontier was a safe place to live.

The Texas Rangers still exist today and are occasionally called on to assist Texas law-enforcement officials.

Although rangers were basically used in areas where no state had yet been formed, the Texas Rangers were not the only ranger organization to exist in the Old West. There was also a smaller group that became known as the Arizona Rangers.

In 1901 the Arizona legislature quietly approved a bill allowing the governor to organize a company

Ben McCulloch came to Texas from Tennessee in 1835. He was a captain of the Texas Rangers and later became a brigadier general in the Confederate army during the Civil War.

The Arizona Rangers were patterned after the Texas Rangers. They hunted down outlaws and helped to maintain order throughout the Arizona Territory.

of fourteen men for the pursuit and arrest of criminals. Burton C. ("Cap") Mossman was the first captain of the Arizona Rangers and is well remembered for capturing a vicious outlaw, Augustin Chacon. But the most famous captain of the Arizona Rangers was Thomas H. Rynning, who reorganized the rangers and, in 1903, persuaded the legislature to authorize more men. This resulted in the formation of the legendary "twenty-six men."

The Arizona Rangers were much like the Texas Rangers in that they wore no uniforms and worked directly for the territorial government. They hunted down rustlers and murderers alike with great success. Only the best men were chosen to serve as Arizona Rangers. By the time the organization came to an end in 1909, the Arizona Rangers had lost only one officer killed in the line of duty.

Only the bravest and most courageous men were picked to serve as rangers for the states of Arizona and Texas. Their job was to step in whenever things looked bleak and the fighting was the toughest. The small amount of money they received for their efforts was sometimes not even enough to buy bullets for their guns and feed for their horses. But they did what they were called on to do and took great pride in what they accomplished, sometimes giving their lives in the process.

SUMMARY

Many things have changed in the last hundred years. Our way of life is much better and far more advanced than that of our pioneer ancestors. We know more about the world—sometimes too much, it seems—and outer space is our new frontier. But the job of the lawman hasn't changed. We still have marshals and sheriffs whose job it is to catch the bad guys.

However, the laws are now more complicated, and often harder to enforce. Today's lawmen must be more than simply tough; they must be tough-minded. In fact, they often wind up being all things to all people, saving men and women not only from the bad guys but sometimes from themselves.

A symbol of the hundreds of men who were lawmen on the western frontier.

You might wonder if the men in this book didn't have a tougher job than the lawmen of today. In a time when carrying a six-gun was expected of a man, it took a lot more courage and patience to settle an argument with words rather than with guns. However, if there is a lesson to be learned from this book, perhaps it is that lawmen have *always* had a tough job. The laws and methods of law enforcement may have changed over the years, but being a lawman has always required personal courage and bravery above and beyond the call of duty.

We have grown quite a bit as a country and a people. The days of the "town tamers" like "Wild Bill" Hickok and Wyatt Earp are gone now, a part of our history. But we can learn from that history if we look in the right places. For example, if we realize that Hickok and Earp were only *two* of the *hundreds* of men who were lawmen on the frontier one hundred years ago, we will know that bravery and courage were not theirs alone.

Nor do bravery and courage belong to a handful of people today. There are thousands of police officers in this country who perform heroic deeds every day as part of their duties. The trouble is we don't often give these men and women the appreciation they deserve.

Think about it a moment. The next time you see a police officer, tell the person he or she is doing a good job. It's guaranteed that, just like Hickok and Earp, you'll make a friend with those words, and that friend will remember you.

Who knows, you may be talking to a real live hero.

FOR FURTHER READING

Bartholomew, Ed. *Wyatt Earp.* Galveston, Texas: Frontier Books, 1963.
One of the better biographies of this frontier lawman.

Erwin, Allen A. *The Southwest of John H. Slaughter, 1841–1922.* Glendale, California: A. H. Clark, 1968.
The most accurate biography of "Texas John" Slaughter.

Metz, Leon. *Pat Garrett: The Story of a Western Lawman.* Norman, Oklahoma: University of Oklahoma Press, 1983.
An important biography of Pat Garrett.

Miller, Nyle H., and Joseph W. Snell. *Great Gunfighters of the Kansas Cowtowns, 1867–1886.* Lincoln, Nebraska: Bison Books, 1967.
Based on Kansas newspaper reports, this book chronicles Kansas lawmen.

Rosa, Joseph G. *They Called Him Wild Bill.* Rev. ed. Stillwater, Oklahoma: Oklahoma University Press, 1974.
This is the most accurate biography on "Wild Bill" Hickok.

Schoenberger, Dale T. *The Gunfighters.* Caldwell, Idaho: Caxton, 1976.
This book offers brief biographies on Hickok, Earp, and Masterson, as well as others.

Surge, Frank. *Western Lawmen.* Minneapolis: Lerner Publications, 1979.

Tilghman, Zoe A. *Marshal of the Last Frontier.* Glendale, California: A. H. Clark, 1949.
The most accurate biography of this western lawman.

Webb, Walter P. *Texas Rangers: A Century of Frontier Defense.* Rev. ed. Austin, Texas: University of Texas Press, 1965.
A history of the Texas Rangers.

INDEX

ABOUT THE AUTHOR

*James L. Collins is the author
of twenty Western novels,
which he writes under the
pen name Jim Miller. A direct
descendant of Leif Erickson
and Eric the Red, he has
always enjoyed storytelling.
Mr. Collins is also the author
of the Franklin Watts book,*
Exploring the American West.